What Is Matter?

by Lola M. Schaefer

Table of Contents

What Is Matter?

Everything is matter, even you!
Matter is made up of very
small things called atoms.
You cannot see atoms.
But you can see a lot of matter.

Everything you see in this picture is matter.

What Are the Different Kinds of Matter You See Every Day?

There are three main kinds of matter that you use every day.

One kind of matter is solid. Solid matter can be hard or soft. Solid matter always has a shape.

All of these toys are made of solid matter.

Some solids are small and some are big.
A pencil is solid matter that
you can carry.

A bus is solid matter that can carry you.

Another kind of matter is liquid.

Liquids flow. They have no shape of their own. They take the shape of whatever is holding them.

Maple syrup is a liquid. This girl is pouring it on her pancakes.

The water in this pool is liquid matter. You can swim in it.

The third kind of matter is gas.

Gases have no shape. They fill up open spaces. Most gases are clear.

Gas is filling up the balloon. Gas makes the balloon get bigger.

Gases are always around us.
The air is made of gases.

Some drinks have bubbles.
These bubbles are gases.

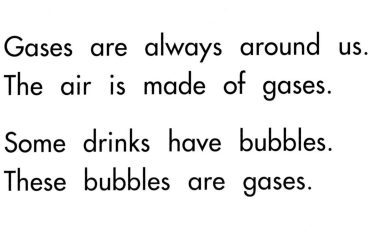

Can Matter Change?

Yes, matter can change. Heating
and cooling can change one form
of matter into another. Solids
can change into liquids. When ice cream
melts, it changes from solid to liquid.

solid

liquid

Liquids can change into gases.
When water boils, it gives off steam.
Steam is a kind of gas.

gas

Liquids can change into solids.
When liquid water freezes,
it becomes solid ice.

liquid

In summer, people can swim in this lake.

solid

In winter, people can skate on this lake.

How Can You Change Matter from Liquid to Solid?

1 Get some juice.

2 Pour the juice into an ice cube tray.

3 Put the tray in the freezer.

4 Wait for three hours.

5 Take the tray
out of the freezer.

6 Pop the cubes
out of the tray.

7 Enjoy!

Glossary

atoms (A-tumz): very small parts of something

flow (FLOH): to move in a stream, like water being poured

freeze (FREEZ): to get cold and become solid, like ice

gas (GAS): a kind of matter that moves and fills up the space around it

liquid (LIH-kwid): a kind of matter that is poured, like water

matter (MA-ter): anything that has weight and takes up space

shape (SHAPE): form

solid (SAH-lid): a kind of matter that is hard or soft and has a shape

space (SPASE): an open place in which all matter is found

Index